John Garst

Delia

OCCASIONAL PAPERS IN FOLKLORE

No. 2

JOHN GARST

Delia

CAMSCO Music
145 Hickory Corner Rd., E. Windsor, NJ 08520
www. camscomusic.com

Loomis House Press
www.loomishousepress.com

ISBN 978-1-935243-88-5

This series of occasional papers in folklore is edited by Ed Cray (cray@usc.edu)

"Delia" (Laws I 5, one of the "Ballads of the Negro") has enjoyed a number of both American and Bahamian field and[1, 2] commercial recordings. Although many versions are fragmentary, that of Will Winn, a "colored troubadour" of the South and West, tells a complete story: Delia agrees to marry Coonie. When she changes her mind, Coonie shoots and kills her. He runs away but is caught, tried, and sentenced to ninety-nine years in prison.[3]

The ballad was first recovered in America in Newton County, Georgia, between 1906 and 1908, as "One Mo' Rounder Gone."[4]

Rubber-tired buggy, double-seated hack,
Well, it carried po' Delia to graveyard, failed to bring her back,
Lawdy, one mo' rounder gone.

Delia's mother weep, Delia's mother mourn,
She wouldn't have taken it so hard if po' girl had died at home,
Well, one mo' ole rounder gone.

Yes, some give a nickel, some give a dime,
I didn't give nary red cent, fo' she was no friend o' mine,
Well, its one mo' rounder gone.

By 1927 it was known in the Bahamas as "Delia Gone," and Bahamians insisted it was based on a local incident.[5]

Tony shot his Delia on a Christmas night
First time he shot her she bowed her head and died—
Delia gone, one more round! Delia gone,
Delia gone, one more round! Delia gone.

Send for the doctor, doctor came too late,
Send for the minister to lay out Delia straight.

Delia's mudder dressed herself in brown,
Went to the cemetery to see her daughter laid down.

Rubber tired buggy, double-seated hack,
Take my Delia to de graveyard an' never brought her back.

Tony axed the jailer, "What is my time?"
"Sixty-four years in ——— ———'s mine."

Sixty-four years, that ain't no time!
Old Joe Bagstack is servin' ninety an' nine!

All you gamblers that likes to bet,
Come on down to de courthouse and witness Delia's death.

The Bahamian belief in a local incident was still strong in 2004.[6]

"Delia" seems to have died out in America by about 1950, but in 1952 it came again as a Bahamian recording, "Delia Gone," by Blind Blake Alphonso Higgs.[7] A great many American recordings followed during the "great folk scare" of the late 1950s and 1960s.[8] With a 1993 version by Bob Dylan, based largely on recordings by Blind Willie McTell, and a 1994 recording of a darkly rewritten version by Johnny Cash, the ballad became firmly fixed in American popular music.[9,10]

Since most American ballads are based on historical incidents,[11] it is likely that Delia was a historical person. If so, who was she, and who killed her? Why?

Delia Discovered

Robert Winslow Gordon wrote in 1928 to Carl Engel, chief of the Music Division of the Library of Congress, that he had traced the ballad to its origin in Savannah, Georgia.[12]

I am tracing... the "Cooney Killed Delia" song—one which will be of the greatest importance in clearing up just how folksong starts and how it spreads. With the assistance of Chief of Detectives McCarthy of Savannah, who has loaned me plainclothes men and in every way aided my search, I have combed the Savannah underworld of the Yamacraw section and have obtained the first hand facts of the murder. Many false clues had to be eliminated, for all I had at first to go on was the first names of the principals, Delia and "Cooney" a nickname. Got the dope at last, interviewed and photographed Delia's mother, had copied fifty pages of court records, discovered over twenty different versions of the song, etc., etc., etc. Still going on with this. More later!!

Engel was Gordon's boss at the Library of Congress. In a letter of November 1928, the year Gordon established the Archive of American Folksong, he gave the name of Delia's killer, Moses Houston, and stated that he then had twenty-eight texts, "no two alike, all fragmentary and garbled."[13] In Georgia, "Houston" is usually pronounced "HOWSS-tun."

Gordon never published his "Delia" discoveries, and most of his relevant papers appear to have been lost. The search for Delia had to start over.[14]

DELIA REDISCOVERED

One version of "Delia" indicates a time frame.[15]

> Nineteen hundred,
> Nineteen hundred and one;
> Death of po' Delia,
> Has jes' now begun.
> > Lil and Babe McClintock Clinton, South Carolina, 1923

Indeed, an article about a pending trial appeared in March 1901.[16]

TO BE TRIED FOR MURDER.

Moses Houston Will Face a Jury for the Killing of Delia Green.

Moses Houston will be placed on trial for the crime of murder in Chatham Superior Court this morning. Judge Seabrook will preside at the trial.

Houston shot and killed a girl, Delia Green, on Christmas Eve of last year. The shooting occurred on Harrison Street, near Laurel, in Yamacraw, and from the evidence of the state's witnesses, seems to have been entirely unprovoked.

The girl, who was but 14 years old, had been accepting the somewhat ardent attentions of Houston for several months, and he had come to think that the whole matter had been settled, and that he was entitled to be favored over all others.

On the night of the homicide when, possibly, his brain was somewhat inflated with Christmas good cheer, he went to the girl and manifested a greater claim of proprietorship over her than she cared to endure. She resented it and denied, somewhat emphatically, that he had any claim on her whatever.

Maddened by this treatment Houston, according to the evidence of the witnesses, drew a revolver and shot the girl in the left groin. She died on the following afternoon. Houston was arrested by bystanders and turned over to the police. He was indicted for murder by the grand jury of the last term of the Superior Court.

The defendant will be represented today by Mr. Raiford Falligant, while Solicitor General W. W. Osborne will prosecute for the state.

Coonie's lawyer, Raiford Falligant, was fresh out of school, having received a law degree from The University of Georgia in 1899.[17] (He would become a juvenile court judge. Perhaps his early experience with Coonie steered him in that direction.)

According to her death certificate,[18] Delia died about four hours after she was shot, not "on the following afternoon," as stated in the article. She was shot late Christmas Eve and died at 3:00 a.m. on Christmas day.

An earlier news report identifies the killer as "Coony Houston."[19] This is the only occurrence of the nickname in a contemporary newspaper.

Relevant historical material includes several other news articles,[20-25] a "Brief of Evidence" presented at Coonie's trial,[26] pardon and parole material,[27] and Delia Green's death certificate.[28] All summaries and quotations of testimony given here are from the "Brief of Evidence."[29] Minor errors and irregularities (e.g., spelling, punctuation) in testimony and news articles are corrected without comment. Two previous reports on "Delia" are based largely on the present research.[30, 31]

YAMACRAW

Savannah lies against the southern bank of the Savannah River, which flows east. In 1898 it was a city of 65,000.[32] The streets of the Historic District form a rectangular grid beginning near the waterfront, and extending southward between West and East Broad Streets. West Broad Street has since been renamed "Martin Luther King Jr. Boulevard."

Yamacraw is a small part of Savannah, about a fifth of a square mile, adjacent to the northwestern corner of the Historic District and separated from it by West Broad Street. Historically, it is a poverty-ridden and violent black neighborhood.[33]

The residence of Willie and Emma West, where Delia Green was shot, was at 509 Harrison Street.[34] Delia lived at 113 Ann Street, about 350 feet from the West house. Coonie lived a few blocks west at 122 Farm Street, about 900 feet from the West house.

Ann Street still exists, and so does Farm Street, renamed "Fahm," but Harrison Street has vanished. Most Yamacraw buildings from Delia's time, largely two-story wooden houses, have been replaced. Only one or two historic churches remain.

Prostitution is strongly associated with seaports and poverty. In 1859 Savannah had one prostitute for every thirty-nine men, while New YorkCity had one for every fifty-seven.[35] Yamacraw has been home to many brothels.[36]

DEFENSE

Coonie told the story this way:

STATEMENT OF DEFENDANT.

Christmas Eve night I went to Emma West house about seven o'clock and then I went home and got supper and went back there. I went and knocked at the door. Mr. Willie was standing on the piazza. I went in the house and called for Delia. She was not there then. Willie asked me to go to the Smith and get his pistol and he gave me a ticket and fifty cents to pay for the repairs to it. I went to get it and brought it back with me to the house and I put it under a cloth or napkin. They were all full in the house. They sent me for beer and whiskey. There was a boy there and he got hold of the pistol and in fun we kind of struggled for it. I told him what are you doing with that pistol, and I got it and it went off and struck Delia. It went off when we are funning. They come out of the house and I went to the corner with the pistol in my hand. Willie West came to me and asked me why I had shot Delia. I told him that I did not mean to do it. I told them to send for the doctor and I would pay for it. The policeman came and arrested me. I told him I did not mean to do it. I told Mr. Sweeney that I wanted to have my pants cleaned and for that reason I had on the short ones.

(Coonie wore short pants to his trial. His explanation was in response Sheriff T. J. Sweeney's testimony that he had worn long pants when he was jailed.)

Coonie's statement was supported by the testimony of Willie Mills.

> I know Mose Houston and saw him on Christmas Eve on Harrison street at Emma West house. He was in a crowd of men and women drinking. I was there too, having some fun Christmas Eve, and I saw a boy there. He and Eddie Cohen were skylarking with a pistol and the pistol went off... Nothing happened just before the shooting except drinking beer and going on. I saw the pistol at the time it fired. The two fellows were tussling together. Both of them had hold of it. I do not know who fired the shot.... I did not hear any language passed just before the shooting. There was a dance and shouting going on.... After the pistol went off he stayed there a little while and then went off. She was taken to her mother's house...

CROSS EXAMINATION:

> I came from jail this morning charged with Larceny for robbing an old man. I have been in jail two months. I went with this boy before. I have not talked to him about this case. There was a crowd of women in the room, all in the same room, as many as twenty in the same room, there was a bed and organ there, plenty of chairs there and a trunk. There was plenty of room for a couple to tussle there....

James C. Chisholm testified that he was a gunsmith and that he recalled "a man Willie West, that man with a handkerchief around his neck, bringing a pistol to my shop to be repaired a short time before Christmas, to the best of my knowledge. I think he is the man. I got rid of the pistol by giving it to a young boy who came for it and produced a written order for the pistol. That is the boy, the defendant, I cannot say positively that he is the boy. He looks like the boy to me. It was bordering on Christmas time

[7]

when he brought the order... He was a young looking boy and a small boy." On redirect examination Chisholm said that he was "positive that is the boy who came in my shop for the pistol after my conversation with him this morning and his mentioning to me about a man speaking through his nose."

Defense witness S. Thomas stated, "I am familiar with the character of the house in which Willie West and his sister and wife stay." An objection terminated his further testimony along this line. On cross examination, he stated, "I have been on the gang twice."

In 1911 Raiford Falligant called the West home a "rough house."[37]

> Christmas Eve night about 11 o'clock in the year 1900, when he was only a boy 14 years of age, he got into bad company in a rough house and got to drinking and tussling with another boy over a pistol which went off and hit and killed a girl in the house where all of the parties were drinking... it was done by him not only accidentally, but when he was crazed by drink in boisterous company for the first time in his life... the crowd he was with and in got him drunk.

PROSECUTION

Emma West had hired Delia to scrub. Her job brought her to the West house frequently.

Willie West testified that Coonie shot Delia at about 11:20 PM on Christmas Eve. While Willie West was playing "Rock of Ages" on the organ, and some were singing, Delia was sitting on the bed. Coonie sat next to her on a trunk. Emma West complained to her husband that Coonie was cursing. When Willie West threatened to put him out, Coonie promised to behave and was allowed to stay. This was fifteen minutes or so before the shooting, so it was probably shortly after 11 PM.

Rosella West, Emma West, and Harriet Gordon testified about the conversation between Delia and Coonie. It went something like this:

[Coonie appears to have bragged that he had been intimate with Delia. She protested vigorously.]

COONIE: My little wife is mad with me tonight. She does not hear me. She is not saying anything to me.

DELIA: Stop! Coonie. Don't put your hands on me.

COONIE: You don't know how I love you.

DELIA: You son of a bitch! You have been going with me for four months. You know I am a lady.

COONIE: That is a damn lie. You know I have had you as many times as I have fingers and toes. You have been calling me "husband."

DELIA: You lie!

[Willie West threatened to put Coonie out.]

COONIE: Don't put me out. I know where I am, and I will act better and stop.

WEST: You will have to behave yourself while in here.

Delia went upstairs. By about 11:20 PM most of the crowd had left, and Delia had come back down. She started out the door, saying, "Let us break up." Coonie pulled out a pistol and shot her before she could get out the door. She screamed, fell back on the bed, said "I am shot," and asked to be taken home. She died at home.

Willie West caught up with Coonie on Margaret Street. He did not resist, but he *did* try a bribe: "Willie, turn me loose for five dollars." Willie turned Coonie and the pistol over to a policeman.

The policeman, J. T. Williams, provided brief but damaging testimony at Coonie's trial.

I arrested Mose Houston Christmas Eve night... He made a statement to me about the shooting. He said that he did it. He said that they had had a little row and they were cursing each other. He said he shot her because she called him a son of a bitch...

Coonie was held in jail until his trial in March 1901.

CONTRADICTIONS

Willie West denied that the pistol was his and that he had taken it at a gunsmith to be fixed. James G. Chisholm, gunsmith, identified Willie West as the man whose pistol he repaired and Coonie as the boy who had presented a ticket and picked it up.

Willie West denied that there had been any "struggle" in his house between Coonie and another boy, contradicting Willie Mills. Eddie Cohen, identified by Mills as the boy with whom Coonie had struggled over the pistol, denied being "at Willie West's house when the shooting took place" and that he had struggled with "this boy for any pistol." He had left before the shooting to take a girl home.

Willie West stated that Delia Green was his wife's cousin. According to his wife, Emma, "I am no kin to Delia Green and she is no cousin to me."

Willie Glover testified that Mills had not been there that night. He had seen Mills in a bar as he had walked to the West house.

Willie West, Rosella West, Emma West, and Harriet Gordon all testified that about eight people were present when Delia was shot, contradicting Mills and his "crowd of men and women... as many as twenty" women. Rosella West said that there "had been a crowd there, but not at the time of the shooting." Emma West said that there were "strangers and friends at my house that night." Harriet Gordon stated that the "biggest portion of the people had already gone" and that the "whole crowd," "five or six people," were "standing up trying to get out and go home."

Every prosecution witness who commented on the subject denied that anyone, except possibly Coonie, drank alcohol that night. Rosella West said that she "did not see any drinking. I suppose they were all sober. I was." Emma West testified, "We were all sober, every one of us. Mose looked as if he had been drinking." Instead of drinking and partying, they had been standing around the organ singing "Rock of Ages" when Coonie shot Delia.

VERDICT AND SENTENCE

In 1900 there was no juvenile justice system in Georgia. Coonie was tried as an adult. For a conviction of murder, with a recommendation of mercy from the jury, the sentence was life in prison.

A news account appeared the day after his trial.[38]

THANKED THE JUDGE

MOSES HOUSTON, GIVEN LIFE IMPRIS-ONMENT, NEVER FLINCHED.

CONVICTED OF MURDER

⸱KILLED DELIA GREEN CHRISTMAS EVE AND MUST PAY PENALTY.

He Is but 15 Years Old and His Youth Served toSave His Neck—Jury Accompanied Its Verdict With a Recommendation to Mercy. Houston's Victim a Girl of Less Than His Own Age—He Took the Ordeal of the Trial Without Turning a Hair—Thanked the Judge When Sentenced to Penitentiary for Life.

"Thank you, sir." This was the response made by Moses Houston, a 15-year-old negro boy, to Judge Seabrook, when the latter sentenced him to spend the remainder of his life in the penitentiary, for the willful murder of Delia Green.

Sentence was imposed at 6:30 o'clock yesterday afternoon and, thus relieved of the necessity of further attendance in the court room, Houston pranced gaily out. He was in charge of a bailiff, but this additional restraint had no effect upon his temper. He was as calm and as debonair as if the experience through which he had just passed was a matter of every day occurrence and of no particular importance.

When he was arraigned in the Superior Court yesterday morning, the youth of the prisoner was the most striking feature of the case. He wore short trousers and had the round cheerful countenance of many mulattoes. He seemed to be rather above the average of negro intelligence and certainly gave no outward indication of being possessed of the "abandoned and malignant heart," which the law says shall be inferred to exist when a killing is committed under circumstances such as surrounded that with which he was charged....

...a verdict of guilty, with a recommendation to mercy, was returned.

Houston was directed to stand up. His nerve never faltered and he faced Judge Seabrook with perfect composure and without any evidence whatever of emotion.

"Houston," said Judge Seabrook, "you have been indicted and tried for the crime of murder. The jury has seen fit to accompany its verdict with a recommendation to mercy, and it now becomes my duty to impose the sentence directed by the law. I perform this duty with some pain and some reluctance; I dislike to condemn one of your youth and apparent intelligence to life imprisonment. In so doing I exhort you to be a man, even in confinement, to repent of your past evil deeds and strive to earn the confidence and respect of those placed in authority over you." The formal sentence of imprisonment for life was then imposed.

Houston's mother, an old black woman of respectable appearance, broke down and sobbed bitterly. Not so the boy himself, for he thanked Judge Seabrook gaily as he was conducted out of the court room.

While he was sitting in the sheriff's office, one of the deputies asked him how he liked the verdict and sentence: "I don't like it at all," was the answer, "but I guess I'll have to stand it."

PRISON

What little we know of Coonie's time in prison comes from news articles and his clemency file. On February 9, 1904, he escaped "from the camps of the Chattachoochee Brick Company, located at the river... Eighteen years of age, yellow skin and of chunky build, round face and small eyes and weighs about 130 pounds. He is 5 feet, 4 or 5 inches tall."[39]

Captain James W. English, a distinguished Confederate veteran who had been the mayor of Atlanta, founded the Chattahoochee Brick Company in 1878. It became the "biggest and arguably most abusive buyer of forced laborers in Georgia."[40] Under very favorable terms, English leased convicts from the State of Georgia. Convict laborers, who had little value, were routinely abused: "one dies, get another."[41]

After his escape, Coonie had more trouble. He went to Harrisburg, Pennsylvania, under the name "George Carl." In 1905 he was incarcerated in the Dauphin County Jail, where he remained until August 1908, when he was returned to Atlanta.[42]

In 1911 Raiford Falligant began preparations for a clemency appeal.[43] On May 26, 1911, Warden J. H. McGwier, Jefferson, Georgia, wrote to Jane Houston, "...your son Mose Houston is in the very best of health and makes me a model prisoner." In September 1911 several officers and guards at the State Convict Camp, Commerce, Georgia, wrote describing Coonie's good behavior and recommending his pardon. In February 1912 Jane Houston wrote that she needed her son Mose Houston to help the family earn a living. Falligant filed the clemency appeal on April 25, 1912. On October 9, 1912, The Prison Commission of Georgia recommended parole.

A State of Georgia Executive Department memo dated October 28, 1912, possibly prepared for the governor, summarizes the case as follows.

> The only thing advanced in behalf of this man is that he was only fourteen years old when the crime was committed and that no malice was proven. He claims it was an accident.
>
> The boy killed a girl on Christmas night, but the trial record does not bear out the claim of accident. It is rather a case of dare-deviltry.
>
> He presents a good record as a prisoner.

Coonie served over twelve years. On October 15, 1913, Governor John M. Slaton approved his parole. Three days later Raiford Falligant wrote that a job was available for Mose Houston at the "colored Laurel Grove Cemetery," where Delia was buried.[44]

In the 1918 Savannah City Directory, Moses Houston is listed as living with his mother at 113 Farm Street and working at "Sav. W. & C. Co." His 1918 draft card, dated September 12, lists him as a porter living at a different address. In 1919 and 1921 a Mose Houston, wife Eva, is listed, in 1921 as a machinist. This may be Coonie.

Gordon wrote in 1928 that he had "trailed Moses Houston to the penitentiary and out again, through more police trouble, and finally to New York City. The negroes *say* he died there a year or so ago. I have uncovered the supposed 'author' of the song, one 'Butch Larkin' and trailed him also to New York."[45]

Coincidentally, and curiously enough, in April 1913 the body of Mary Phagan was found in a pencil factory in Atlanta. Two years later, Leo Frank was convicted and sentenced to death. In June 1915 Governor Slaton, believing Frank to be innocent and knowing that his action would end his political career in Georgia, commuted the sentence to life in prison. He told his wife, "…it may mean my death or worse, but I have ordered the sentence commuted." It is said that Mrs. Slaton kissed her husband and said, "I would rather be the widow of a brave and honorable man than the wife of a coward."[46] In the aftermath of his decision, incredible abuse was heaped on Slaton. A few days after he commuted Frank's sentence, Slaton left office. In August Frank was taken from his jail cell by a mob and lynched.[47]

"Mary Phagan" (Laws F 20) describes the crime from the perspective that Frank was the killer. Thus, Governor Slaton is connected with at least two traditional ballads.

What Really Happened?

There was a lot of lying at the trial. Coonie and Willie Mills could have agreed on their stories while they were in jail together. Willie West, Rosella West, Emma West, and Harriet Gordon had plenty of opportunity to have done the same.

Willie West denied owning the pistol. The testimony of the gunsmith leaves little doubt that he did own it and that Coonie had picked it up for him.

The Wests portrayed their home as a kind of religious center. The party had been a hymn-singing. There was no drinking, except possibly by Coonie. Surely no jurors believed this part of their story.

The key witness was policeman J. T. Williams, who testified that Coonie told him that he had shot Delia because she had called him a "son of a bitch" and that "he would do it again." This verifies the more detailed stories, to the same effect, of the Wests and Harriet Gordon.

It really *was* dare-deviltry, aggravated by alcohol and jealousy.[48]

Was Delia a Prostitute?

It is unfortunate that we do not know what S. Thomas would have said about the "character" of the West house. Knowing that he was a defense witness and that Falligant later called it a "rough house," we can surmise that Thomas would have testified to regular illegal activities there.

Willie West testified, "Nobody stayed at my house except my wife and another fellow who stayed upstairs, and my sister. Delia Green was there helping my wife, washing dishes… She was frequently at my house." The question that elicited this response may have been prompted by a defense belief or suspicion that the house was a brothel. This could explain why Cooney and Willie Mills referred to the "Emma West house" instead of the "Willie West house." Perhaps Emma was a madam, consistent with Willie Mills's statement that there was a "crowd of women… as many as twenty."

Coonie could have been dismayed that Delia had become a prostitute. Other men have killed prostitutes they loved and of whom they were jealous. For example, Louis "Bull" Martin killed Ella Speed in a New Orleans brothel in 1894 because she would not confine her attentions to him.[49]

Whether or not Delia was in the profession, the West house may have been an entertainment center featuring gambling, music, drink, and women. It had two stories and was equipped with an organ in a large, downstairs room. Typically, downstairs parlors were where customers were received and entertained with conversation, drink, gambling, music and dancing. For intimacy, customers would go upstairs to a woman's room. (In a legendary prank, a male caller who dials the wrong number and asks for "Mabel" is told, "I'm sorry. She's upstairs with a customer.")

BALLAD VS FACT

No testimony or news account mentions Delia's possible involvement with other boys or men, as is implied in some versions of the ballad. For example, Blind Willie McTell sang, "You love that old rounder / But you don't love me,"[50] and Zora Neale Hurston collected the following stanza.[51]

> Mama, oh, mama, how could I stand
> When all around my bedside was full of married men
> So she's gone, she's dead and gone

No testimony or news account suggests that Delia refused Coonie's offer of marriage.[52] The closest to this is the testimony that Coonie considered

Delia to be his common-law wife, which Delia denied vehemently. Delia's two-timing, Coonie's desire to marry, and his thanking the judge all appear in an unusual version of "Delia Gone" that is marked by humorous word-play.[53]

1   Miss Delia, she two-timed her
Tony Saturday night,
And on this date she met her fate,
He shot her down at sight.

Chorus: Delia gone, one more round,
Delia gone!

2   He brought her a cocktail,
The very best in town,
But she refused to down the shot
And so he shot her down.

3   He wanted to marry
But she preferred to be loose,
She did not want a goose to cook
And so he cooked her goose.

4   So Tony was locked up,
The judge refused to set bail,
For such a crime, he should do time,
Say, 99 years in jail.

5   Then Tony said "Thank You",
"Your honor treated me fine."
He knew the judge could well have said:
Nine hundred ninety-nine.

Stanzas 2 and 3 are so unusual that this version could be thought spurious, that is, not a representative of a real tradition but instead someone's humorous rewrite. The last stanza forces reconsideration. This is the only version to mention that Coonie thanked the judge.

Delia's cursing Coonie appears in the ballad several times. Zora Neale Hurston collected a historically accurate stanza around Fernandina, Florida, about 100 miles from Savannah.[54] Here, "tell me 'bout my mama" is a euphemism for "call me a son of a bitch."

> Coonie told Delia on a Christmas Eve night,
> If you tell me 'bout my mama I'm sho going to take your life.
> She's dead, she's dead and gone.

Other accurate elements are found in the Blind Blake's "Delia Gone."

> 5   On Monday Tony was arrested,
> On Tuesday his case was tried,
> The juryman brought him down guilty,
> He began to rollin' his goo-goo eyes.

Christmas Eve, 1900, when Coonie was arrested, was indeed a Monday. His trial, however, was on a Thursday, not a Tuesday. Whether or not he rolled "his goo-goo eyes," he did act gaily at the end of his trial.[55] In the version from the Bahamas given by Defries, rolling his goo-goo eyes is attributed to the parson.[56]

Blind Willie McTell sang that Delia was a "gambling girl" who "gambled all around."[57,58] This has no basis in testimony or news accounts. Perhaps the idea was transferred from "Frankie," in which Albert/Johnny is a gambling man.[59]

Some versions of "Delia," including McTell's, imply that Delia did not die at home. In fact, she did.

McTell and Will Winn sang that Delia's mother took a trip out West.[60] This could be a garbled statement derived from the fact that Delia was at the home of Willie West when she was shot.

Winn correctly sang that Coonie asked the governor for a pardon.

If there were a way to know which ballad statements were true and which weren't, one could construct a fair picture of the crime described in

"Delia." This could not be done with "Ella Speed," for which the facts of the case bear little resemblance to those given in ballads.[61]

LINEARITY AND NODALITY

Gordon traced the ballad to "Butch Larkin," who disappeared in New York City. According to Will Winn, "Delia" was by a "white minstrel of Dallas, Texas, known as 'Whistlin' Bill Ruff.'" However, Milling thought it "too typically Negroid to admit of this explanation."[62]

Most of Winn's twenty-three stanzas tell the story linearly. Such sustained linearity is not often found black ballad singing. "Because they emphasize character and situation, in contrast to white ballads, which usually concentrate on events, the Negro ballads seem to be highly personal expressions of characteristic racial attitudes."[63]

Many versions of "Delia" are typical nodal ballads, which are more heavily represented in black than white American singing.[64-67] In a nodal ballad, there is a "near-total suppression of narrative sequence in favor of a series of comments upon a story which must in large part be inferred from these comments."[68]

Even though Winn's "Delia" is largely a linear ballad, some features of nodal ballads are present. One is that the first stanza is out of temporal order. Another is its inclusion of floating stanzas.

Nodal ballads are fluid. They often incorporate floating stanzas. Laws gives examples for Winn's "Delia," "Duncan and Brady," and "Stagolee."[69]

> Delia, Delia
> Why didn't you run,
> See dat desparado
> Had a forty fo' smokeless gun. ("Delia")

> Brady, Brady
> Why didn't you run,
> When you saw that Duncan
> Had a forty-four gun? ("Duncan and Brady")

"Some give a nickel
Some give a dime,
Help to bury
This body of mine." ("Delia")

Some give a nickel,
some give a dime,
I didn't give a red copper cent,
'cause he's no friend o' mine. ("Stagolee")

Further, the "silver cup" stanza is found in Winn's "Delia" and "White House Blues." [70, 71]

Coonie went to Atlanta
Drinkin' from a silver cup,
Po' li'l' Delia's in the cemetery
I hope to never wake up. ("Delia")

Roosevelt's in the White House,
drinkin' out of a silver cup,
McKinley's in the graveyard,
never waked up. ("White House Blues")

Perhaps the best interpretation is that an original linear ballad was transformed in the hands of black singers to a typical nodal ballad. Winn's version could then be seen as an intermediate form. These considerations suggest, but do not require, a white author.

"Delia" and "McKinley"

President McKinley was assassinated in September 1901, nearly nine months after Delia Green's death. At the bottom of a typed text of "Delia" obtained from "D. W., Darien, Ga., July 9, 1927," Robert W. Gordon wrote, "Same tune as McKinley. Sung in the spring of the same year. McKinley shot in the fall." [72] Although Milling wrote that Winn's tune "could not be found at all," Gordon recognized it as the usual tune of "McKinley," or

"White House Blues." Tunes evolve, but in both America and the Bahamas, "Delia" tunes are recognizable variants of the "McKinley" tune.

"Delia" and "McKinley" texts are related as well, having stanzas and phrases in common. In addition, a version of "Delia" sung by Lil and Mc-Clintock uses "Buffalo, sweet Buffalo" as a tag line.[73] The tag line of McKinley is often "From Buffalo to Washington" or "In Buffalo, in Buffalo."[74] "McKinley" could have been patterned after "Delia." However, cat yronwode points out a strong resemblance to "The Battleship of Maine," a song about the Spanish-American war of 1898, and Jonathan Lighter finds a likeness to "There'll be a Hot Time in the Old Town Tonight" (music by Theo. A. Metz, 1896).[75, 76]

In America, only blacks are known to have sung "Delia" before 1952, with the single exception of Datron Brown, Bishopville, SC, a "white boy."[77] Conversely, although "McKinley" has been sung by blacks in Virginia and Delaware,[78] it is primarily a song of whites, currently a staple in the bluegrass repertoire.

ONE MORE ROUND

In America, before 1952, "Delia" appears with many tag lines: "One more rounder gone," "All I had done gone," "She's gone, po' gal, she's gone," "She's dead, she's dead and gone," "An' Lawd you gone, you gone, Delia, you gone," "Yes, all the friends I got is gone," etc. "Delia('s) gone, one more round, Delia('s) gone" is not among them. It appears to have originated in the Bahamas.

Tag lines that arrived in the Bahamas as "one more rounder gone" and "you gone, Delia, you gone," or something like them, appear to have mutated to "Delia gone, one more round, Delia gone." "One more rounder" became "one more round," an easy transition that may have been facilitated by Bahamian speech or culture. "One more round" may mean "sing it again." If so, the second "Delia gone" fulfills this imperative. "One more round" could also be a call for another drink, a toast to Delia.

After 1952, "one more round" versions became abundant in American popular music, reflecting the influence of Blind Blake's recording.[79] America originated the ballad and sent it to the Bahamas. The Bahamas modified it and sent it back to America, where Bahamanian versions ("one more

[21]

round") are now better known, probably, than American versions ("one more rounder").

LAUREL GROVE CEMETERY SOUTH

The black section of Laurel Grove Cemetery, where Delia Green is buried, is now known as Laurel Grove Cemetery South. A freeway divides the black and white sections.

A cemetery inventory does not mention Delia. It seems likely that she was buried in the paupers' area near the north end of the cemetery. At that time, grave markers for paupers were not allowed.

Views of Laurel Grove Cemetery South can be seen on the Web.[80] The soil is sandy and the trees drip with Spanish moss. Along the western border is a lovely small pond, usually filled with waterfowl.[81] Delia rests in beauty.

REFERENCES AND NOTES

1. Laws, G. Malcolm, Jr. *Native American Balladry.* Revised edition. Philadelphia, Pennsylvania: American Folklore Society, 1964.

2. Cowley, John. "West Indies Blues." *Nobody Knows Where the Blues Come From: Lyrics and History.* Ed. Robert Springer. Jackson, Mississippi: University Press of Mississippi, 2006. 187-263.

3. Milling, Chapman J. "Delia Holmes—a Neglected Negro Ballad." *Southern Folklore Quarterly* 1.4 (1937): 3-8.

4. Odum, Howard W. "Folk-Song and Folk-Poetry as Found in the Secular Songs of the Southern Negroes." *Journal of American Folklore* 24.94 (1911): 351-96.

5. McCutcheon, John T., et al. *The Island Song Book.* Chicago: Privately printed at The Chicago Tribune tower, 1927.

6. Newton, M. Gary. Personal communication with the author. 2004. When I learned that Gary Newton was going to vacation in the Bahamas at the end of December, 2004, I asked him to ask Bahamians about "Delia Gone." He found several who knew the song and who were certain that it was based on a local event.—JG

7. Higgs, Blake Alphonso (Blind Blake). *A Third Album of Bahamian Songs By "Blind Blake" And the Royal Victoria Hotel "Calypso" Orchestra.* LP. ALP-6. "Delia Gone" is band 2, side 2. Art Records, Inc., Miami, FL, 1952. See also Patterson, Massie, and Sammy Heyward, Eds. *Calypso Folk Sing.* New York: Ludlow Music, Inc., 1963. Copyright 1952 and 1954 by Hollis Music, Inc., New York. 26-27.

8. HighRoad. "The Great Folk Scare". Seattle, Washington, 2002. Zipcon Internet Services. May 30 2012. <http://www.zipcon.com/~highroad/folkscare.html>

9. Dylan, Bob. *World Gone Wrong.* CD. Columbia CK 57590. Sony Music Entertainment Inc., New York, 1993.

10. Cash, Johnny. *American Recordings.* CD. American 9 45520-2. American Recordings, Burbank, California, 1994.

11. Laws, *Balladry*, ref. 1, p 48.

12. Kodish, Debra. *Good Friends and Bad Enemies: Robert Winslow Gordon and the Study of American Folksong.* Urbana, Illinois: University of Illinois Press, 1986. 163.

13. Gordon, Robert W. Letter to Carl Engel. November 15. 1928. *Folk-Songs of America: The Robert Winslow Gordon Collection*, 1922-1932. The American Folklife Center. Library of Congress. Washington, DC.

14. I am indebted to John Cowley for suggesting that I pursue "Delia."—JG.

15. Milling, "Delia," ref. 3.

16. *Savannah Morning News.* "To Be Tried for Murder." March 14. 1901: 10. Savannah, Georgia.

17. Harden, William. *A History of Savannah and South Georgia.* 1913. Chicago and New York: The Lewis Publishing Company. Reprint: Atlanta, Georgia: Cherokee Publishing Company, 1969. 679-81.

18. Green, Delia. *Physicians' Certificate of the Cause of Death.* Savannah, Georgia: Chatham County Health Department, 1900.

19. *Savannah Morning News.* "Shot Because Rejected." December 26. 1900.

20. *Savannah Press.* "Boy Killed Girl." December 26. 1900: 5.

21. ———. "Boy Charged with Murder." March 14. 1901: 1.

22. *Savannah Morning News.* "Thanked the Judge." March 15. 1901: 3.

23. *Atlanta Constitution, The.* "Negro Boy's Life Sentence." March 15. 1901: 2. Atlanta, Georgia. ProQuest Historical Newspapers Atlanta Constitution (1868-1945).

24. ———. "Life Convict Makes Escape." February 10. 1904: 5. Atlanta, Georgia. ProQuest Historical Newspapers Atlanta Constitution (1868-1945).

25. ———. "Free for Four Years. Convict Is Recaptured." August 28. 1908: 4. Atlanta, Georgia. ProQuest Historical Newspapers Atlanta Constitution (1868-1945).

26. Hartridge, Walter C., Solicitor General, F. J. C. of Ga. *Brief of Evidence. State Vs. Mose Houston.* Savannah, GA: Chatham Superior Court. March Term, 1901. Moses Houston Clemency File, Georgia Department of Archives and History, Atlanta, Georgia.

27. Houston, Mose. 1912. Clemency File, Georgia Department of Archives and History, Atlanta, Georgia.

28. Green death certificate, ref. 18.

29. Hartridge, *Brief,* ref. 26.

30. Garst, John. "Delia." *Blues & Rhythm.* 189 (May) (2004): 8-10.

31. Wilentz, Sean. "The Sad Song of Delia Green and Cooney Houston." *The Rose & the Briar.* Eds. Sean Wilentz and Greil Marcus. New York and London: W. W. Norton & Company, 2005. 147-58.

32. Sanborn Map. "Savannah, Georgia". 1898. Sanborn-Perris Map Company Limited. <http://dlg.galileo.usg.edu/sanborn/CityCounty/Savannah1898/>

33. Ball, Kimberly. Letter to the author, February 29. 2000.

34. Willie West's house at 509 Harrison Street is not included in the 1900 census. In that census, Willie and Emma West live at 11 Lumber Street with Willie's mother, Jane West. Willie is a longshoreman. At Delia's address, 113 Ann Street, Adam Singleton, day laborer, lives with his wife Fannie and a lodger, William Jones. City directories give the head of the household as J. (John) or Mingo Singleton. Delia Green does not appear in the census. Jane Houston, widow, lives at 123 Farm Street with Moses Houston and five other children. All of these addresses are in Yamacraw.

35. Ayers, Edward L. *Vengeance and Justice.* New York: Oxford, 1984.

36. Lockley, Timothy James. *Lines in the Sand: Race and Class in Lowcountry Georgia*, 1750-1860. Athens, Georgia: University of Georgia Press, 2001.

37. Falligant, Raiford. *The Petition of Mose Houston.* Savannah, Georgia: State of Georgia, Governor and Pardon Board, 1911. Moses Houston Clemency File, Georgia Department of Archives and History, Atlanta, Georgia.

38. *News,* "Thanked," ref. 22.

39. *Constitution,* "Escape," ref. 24.

40. Blackmon, Douglas A. *Slavery by Another Name: The Re-Enslavement of Black Americans from the Civil War to World War II.* New York: Doubleday, 2008. 1st Anchor Books ed. New York: Anchor Books, 2009.

41. Mancini, Matthew J. *One Dies, Get Another: Convict Leasing in the American South, 1866-1928.* Columbia, South Carolina: University of South Carolina Press, 1996.

42. *Constitution,* "Recaptured," ref. 25.

43. Houston, Clemency, ref. 27.

44. Green death certificate, ref. 18.

45. Gordon to Engel, ref. 13.

46. Dinnerstein, Leonard. *The Leo Frank Case.* Athens: University of Georgia Press, 1987.

47. Kennedy, John F. *Profiles in Courage.* New York: Harper and Row, 1964.

48. Far too frequently, men murder inconveniently pregnant women. Ballads telling these stories serve as cautionary tales. "Delia" is different. She rejected and cursed a jealous drunk. Her ballad can also serve as a cautionary tale.

49. Cowley, John, and John Garst. "Behind the Song ("Ella Speed")." *Sing Out!* 45.1 (2001): 69-70.

50. McTell, Blind Willie. "Delia." Sound recording for the Library of Congress by John A. and Ruby Lomax, Atlanta, Georgia, November 5, 1940. LOC 4070 A2. *Blind Willie McTell 1940.* Vienna, Austria: Document Records BDCD-6001, Band 4. 1990.

51. Bordelon, Pamela, editor. *Go Gator and Muddy the Water: Writings by Zora Neale Hurston from the Federal Writers' Project.* New York: W. W. Norton, 1999. 73.

52. Milling, "Delia," ref. 3.

53. Bayas, Arthur, and Lipton Nemser. *The Best Bluegrass Songbook—Yet!* Carlstadt, New Jersey: Lewis Music Publishing Company, Inc., 1978. 60-61.

54. Bordelon, *Gator*, ref. 51, p 73.

55. *News*, "Thanked," ref. 22.

56. Defries, Amelia. *The Fortunate Islands.* London: Cecil Palmer, 1929.

57. McTell, "Delia," ref. 50.

58. McTell, Blind Willie. *Atlanta Twelve String.* CD. Atlantic 7 82366-2. Recorded 1949. "Little Delia," Band 3, 1992.

59. Lomax, John Avery, and Alan Lomax. *American Ballads and Folk Songs.* New York: Macmillan, 1934. 103-10.

60. Milling, "Delia," ref. 3.

61. Cowley, "Ella Speed," ref. 49.

62. Milling, "Delia," ref. 3.

63. Laws, *Balladry*, ref. 1, p 84.

64. Wilgus, D. K. *Obray Ramsey Sings Folksongs from the Three Laurels.* Prestige/International LP 1320, Liner Notes, 1961.

65. Wilgus, D. K., and Lynwood Montell. "Clure and Joe Williams: Legend and Blues Ballad." *The Journal of American Folklore* 81. No. 322 (Oct.-Dec.) (1968): 295-315.

66. Wilgus, D. K., and Eleanor R. Long. "The Blues Ballad and the Genesis of Style in Traditional Song." *Narrative Folksong, New Directions: Essays in Appreciation of W. Edson Richmond.* Eds. Carol L. Edwards and Kathleen B. Manley. Boulder, Colorado: Westview Press (printer), 1985. 434-82.

67. Oliver, Paul. *Songsters and Saints: Vocal Traditions on Race Records.* Cambridge, New York: Cambridge University Press, 1984. 247.

68. Wilgus, "Blues Ballad," ref. 66.

69. Laws, *Balladry*, ref. 1, 89-91.

70. Milling, "Delia," ref. 3.

71. Lomax, John Avery, et al. *Our Singing Country.* New York: Macmillan, 1941. Mineola, NY: Dover, 2000. 258.

72. Gordon, Robert W. "Cooney Shot Delia." Ax 39, *Robert Winslow Gordon Collection*, Box 9, Folder 4. Division of Special Collections & University Archives, University of Oregon Library System, Eugene, Oregon.

73. Milling, "Delia," ref. 3.

74. Cohen, Norm. Long Steel Rail: *The Railroad in American Folksong.* Second ed. Urbana: University of Illinois Press, 2000. 413-25. First edition: 1981.

75. E-mail communications to <pre-war-blues@yahoogroups.com> and <ballad-l@iulist.indiana.edu>, June 11, 2012.

76. Hayden, Joe, and Theo. A. Metz. "A Hot Time in the Old Town". New York, New York, 1896. Willis Woodward and Company. <http://levysheetmusic.mse.jhu.edu/otcgi/llscgi60>. In the *Lester S. Levy Collection of Sheet Music*, Special Collections at the Sheridan Libraries of The Johns Hopkins University, Baltimore, Maryland.

77. Milling, "Delia," ref. 3.

78. Uncle Ben Collins, Smyrna, Delaware, sang "When McKinley was Shot" for the Library of Congress in 1941, according to Dixon, Godrich, and Rye, *Blues and Gospel Records 1890-1943*, Fourth Edition, 1997. Sticks McGhee included a stanza of "McKinley" in his 1946 recording of "Railroad Bill." I am indebted to Chris Smith for the McGhee information. He and Guido van Rijn drew my attention to the Uncle Ben recording. Two "White House Blues" recordings by Virginia blacks, Big Sweet Lewis Hairston and Howard Twine, are online at the Digital Library of Appalachia: <http://dla.acaweb.org/cdm/search/

searchterm/white%20house%20blues/order/nosort> They were recorded in 1977 and 1978, respectively, but they appear to represent old traditions.

79. Higgs, "Delia Gone," ref. 7.

80. King-Tisdell Cottage Foundation. "Laurel Grove Cemetery South". 2003. June 1, 2012. <http://www.kingtisdell.org/laurel.htm>

81. To reach Laurel Grove Cemetery South, go south from the Historic District to 37th Street. Turn right (west) and follow the road straight into the cemetery gate.

When John Garst retired in 1997 from The University of Georgia, where he had been a professor of chemistry, he turned his attention to American folk hymns ("Wayfaring Stranger," "Man of Constant Sorrow") and ballads ("Ella Speed," "Delia," "John Henry.") He and his wife Edna, who live in Athens, Georgia, are the proud parents of a daughter who is a lung-cancer specialist.

CPSIA information can be obtained
at www.ICGtesting.com
Printed in the USA
JSHW031942080123
35629JS00004B/84